TROMBONE/BARITONE B.C.

ACCENT ON Christmas & Holiday ENSEMBLES

John O'Reilly and Mark Williams

Duets and trios for flexible instrumentation
correlated with *ACCENT ON ACHIEVEMENT*, Book 1

Dear Band Student:

Congratulations on becoming a member of the **band!** Another fun way to make music is to play in an **ensemble.** When you perform duets and trios with your friends, you become even more skilled as a musician. This book features Christmas and holiday ensembles correlated with specific pages in *Accent on Achievement, Book 1*, and is playable by students working in any first-year band method. You can play these ensembles with like instruments or with any combination of mixed instruments. Have fun making music together as you perform with *Accent on Christmas and Holiday Ensembles!*

TABLE OF CONTENTS

Title	Page	Correlates with Book 1 Page
Jingle Bells	2	12
Jolly Old St. Nicholas	3	13
Up on the Housetop	4	13
Good King Wenceslas	5	21
African Noel	6	21
Hanukkah, Hanukkah	8	21
Bring a Torch, Jeanette, Isabella	10	24
Dreydl Song	11	24
We Wish You a Merry Christmas	12	24
O Come, O Come Emmanuel	13	25
Deck the Halls	14	25
Joy to the World	15	25
Away in a Manger	16	25
We Three Kings	17	25
The First Noel	18	25
Angels from the Realms of Glory	19	25
Hark! The Herald Angels Sing	20	30
Angels We Have Heard on High	21	30
Hanukkah, O Hanukkah	22	33
Ding, Dong Merrily on High	23	33
Auld Lang Syne	24	33

Alfred

Copyright © MMIII by Alfred Publishing Co., Inc.
All Rights Reserved.   Printed in USA.

JINGLE BELLS

James Pierpont
(1822–1893)

JOLLY OLD ST. NICHOLAS

Traditional

Up on the Housetop

Benjamin Hanby
(1833–1867)

GOOD KING WENCESLAS

Traditional English Carol
(based on a Swedish Folk Song)

AFRICAN NOEL

Liberian Folk Song

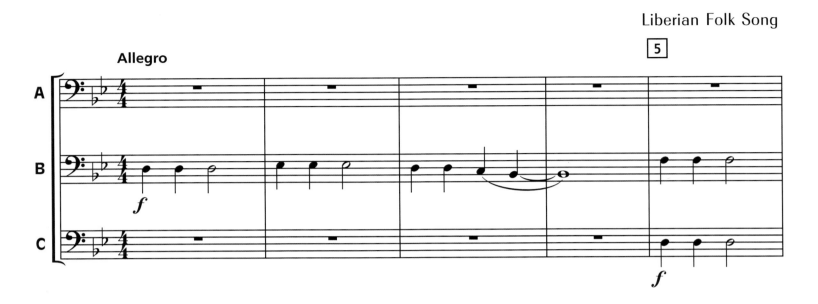

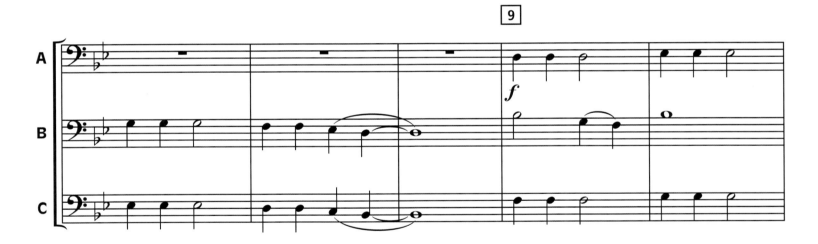

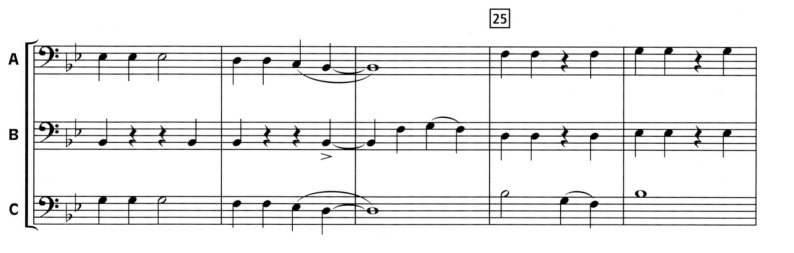

HANUKKAH, HANUKKAH

Traditional

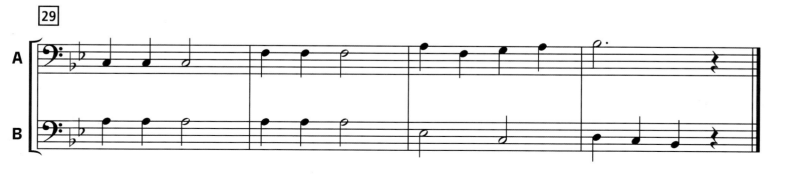

BRING A TORCH, JEANETTE, ISABELLA

French Carol

DREYDL SONG

Traditional Hanukkah Song

WE WISH YOU A MERRY CHRISTMAS

English Folk Song

O Come, O Come Emmanuel

13th-Century Plainsong

DECK THE HALLS

Traditional Welsh Carol

JOY TO THE WORLD

George F. Handel
(1685–1759)

AWAY IN A MANGER

James Murray
(1841–1905)

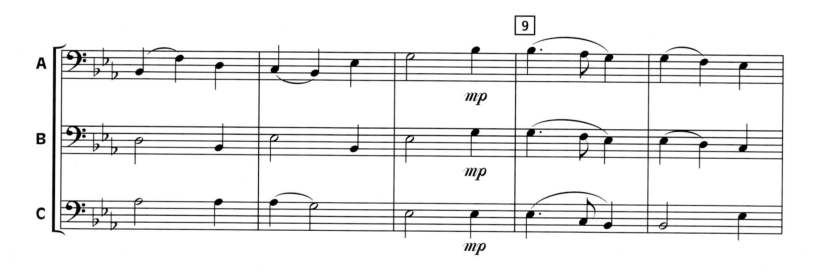

WE THREE KINGS

John Hopkins
(1820–1891)

THE FIRST NOEL

French-English Carol

ANGELS FROM THE REALMS OF GLORY

Henry Smart
(1813–1879)

Hark! The Herald Angels Sing

Felix Mendelssohn
(1809–1847)

ANGELS WE HAVE HEARD ON HIGH

French-English Carol

HANUKKAH, O HANUKKAH

Traditional

DING, DONG MERRILY ON HIGH

Thoinot Arbeau
(1520–1595)

AULD LANG SYNE

Traditional Scottish Air

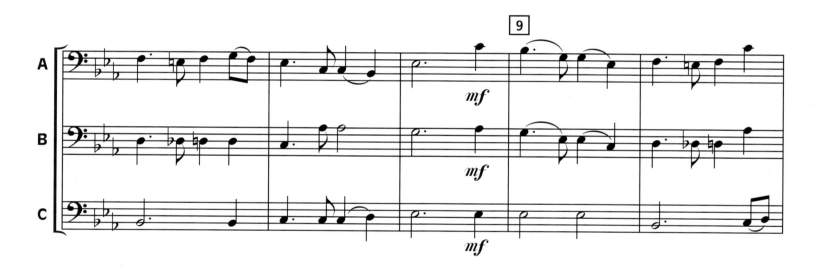